CONTENTS ▪ ▪ ▪ ▪

INTRODUCTION

Suddenly, everybody loved the Beatles. When the band played in concert, police had to hold back crowds of screaming fans – mainly girls. The same thing happened when the band went to a TV or radio studio. One newspaper thought of a new word to describe the country's love of the boys from Liverpool – 'Beatlemania'!

The year was 1963, but Beatlemania was only just beginning. Soon the Beatles had fans all around the world. For the rest of the 1960s, their music led the way. Each record brought new sounds, new ideas.

How did four boys from Liverpool reach this position? What was so special about the Beatles? And why did it all have to end? This book follows the story from their happy early days in Liverpool until the sad end of the most famous group in the world.

■ ■ ▪ ▪

Paul Shipton grew up near Liverpool. He was only seven at the time of the Beatles' last album, but he has always listened to and loved the band. His favourite Beatles album is probably *Revolver*. His favourite song is 'Strawberry Fields Forever' or 'A Day in the Life' – or perhaps 'I Am the Walrus' or 'Hey Jude' or . . . ! He lives in the United States now with his wife and two daughters.

THE UNIVERSITY OF
WINCHESTER

Martial Rose Library
Tel: 01962 827306

To be returned on or before the day marked above, subject to recall.

The Beatles

PAUL SHIPTON

Level 3

Series Editors: Andy Hopkins and Jocelyn Potter

Pearson Education Limited
Edinburgh Gate, Harlow,
Essex CM20 2JE, England
and Associated Companies throughout the world.

ISBN 0 582 512484

First published by Penguin Books 2002

1 3 5 7 9 10 8 6 4 2

Copyright ©Paul Shipton 2002
Colour reproduction by Spectrum Colour Ltd, Ipswich
Design by John Fordham

Printed and bound in Denmark by Norhaven A/S, Viborg

Published by Pearson Education Limited in association with Penguin
Books Ltd, both companies being subsidiaries of Pearson Plc

Photograph acknowledgements:
Rex Features: pp. 1,3, 8, 26, 30, 38 and 40; Redferns: pp. 6, 13,
16, 21, 25, 27, 35, 36 and 39; Camera Press: pp. 11 and 33;
Aquarius: pp.14 and 29.

For a complete list of titles available in the Penguin Readers series please write to your local
Pearson Education office or to: Marketing Department, Penguin Longman Publishing,
80 Strand, London WC2R 0RL.

The End of a Dream

Paul McCartney once said, 'The Beatles were always a great little band – nothing more, nothing less.' Millions of fans around the world disagree with this. To them, the Beatles were a 'great little band' who changed modern music forever.

When the Beatles ended in 1970, people around the world couldn't believe it. John, Paul, George and Ringo all followed their own interests successfully. But all four faced the same question everywhere they went: 'When will you play together again?' The answer always seemed the same – never – but fans could hope and dream.

Then, on 8 December 1980, the dream ended. John Lennon and Yoko Ono were returning home to their building in New York. Mark Chapman was waiting in the shadows. He shouted to John and then he shot the singer in the back and chest. John Lennon died in hospital that night.

The news was met with sadness all around the world. The Beatles could never play together again.

Early Days

The four boys from Liverpool were all born during the Second World War. Life in the northern city wasn't always easy after the war. Most people lived in small houses and many were poor. But like many ports, Liverpool was open to new ideas. Sometimes ships brought something that other places in Britain couldn't get – rock and roll records from the US! For the young people of Liverpool in the 1950s, the exciting sound of rock and roll was an escape from their daily lives.

■ **Richard Starkey** (Ringo Starr) was born in 1940 and grew up in one of Liverpool's poorest areas. He was often ill, and he first played drums in hospital. He bought his first drum around 1956 – just one big drum! He played with a few local bands. Then he joined Rory Storm and the Hurricanes. Around this time, Richard took a new name – 'Ringo'– because of all the rings on his hands.

■ **George Harrison**, the youngest Beatle, was born in 1943. His father was a bus driver, but before that he worked on ships. George loved his father's records from the US. At school, he sat in class drawing pictures of guitars. When he did get his guitar, he practised all the time.

■ **Paul McCartney** was born in 1942, the son of a nurse and a cotton salesman. The family loved music. When Paul was old enough, his father bought him a trumpet. But Paul couldn't play the trumpet and sing at the same time. So he changed the trumpet for a guitar. He sometimes talked about music with a younger boy at his school – George Harrison.

■ **John Lennon** was born in 1940. After his father left, his mother sent the four-year-old boy to his Aunt Mimi and her husband's big house in a pleasant part of Liverpool. John loved rock and roll. He remembered seeing an Elvis Presley film. When the audience screamed, he thought, 'That's a good job!' John's mother loved music too – and she taught her son well. He started a band, the Quarry Men. The name came from his school, Quarry Bank.

One afternoon in July 1957, a friend took Paul to see the Quarry Men at a church garden party. John was singing, but he couldn't remember all the words. This didn't stop him – he sang new words. After the concert, Paul played a song on his guitar for John. Years later, John remembered the meeting. Paul was better than the people in the band, but John was a little worried. What was more important: his own strong position in the group, or a stronger group? He chose the group. Lennon and McCartney were together.

From Liverpool to Hamburg

One day, Paul showed John one of his own songs. After that, John began to write his own musical ideas, and soon the two young men were writing song after song. Sometimes they worked together, sometimes alone. But each of them pushed himself harder because of the other one. This was true during all the Beatles years.

Not long after Paul joined, he told John about his friend George. John wasn't sure – George was only fifteen. But George joined after John heard him play. They were on the top of a bus at the time!

Soon John, Paul and George were playing concerts in Liverpool, but there was a problem. They didn't have a drummer or a bass guitarist. One of John's art-school friends, Stu Sutcliffe, looked like James Dean and he was an artist. When he sold a painting, the boys in the band asked him to buy a bass guitar. Stu wanted to be in a band, but there was one small problem: he couldn't play. Stu often turned his back to the crowds in concerts because of this!

What's in a name?

John and Stu probably thought of the name 'the Beatles', but there are other stories. John wrote that, at twelve years old, he was told the name by a little man. There was a more serious story, too: they heard it in a Marlon Brando film, *The Wild One*. But many years later, Paul McCartney named a 1997 album *Flaming Pie*, for the place where John saw his little man!

People were starting to like the band. The Beatles got a job playing with a rock and roll singer, Johnny Gentle. They toured Scotland under the name the Silver Beetles. For a time, Paul played drums because they couldn't find a drummer. Then, back in Liverpool, they were offered another job. Bands were needed to play in clubs in the German city of Hamburg. The band said yes – but first they needed a drummer. They asked Pete Best, the drummer in another local band (and the owner of some nice drums!). Pete agreed and the band travelled to Germany in the summer of 1960.

To five boys from Liverpool, Hamburg was another world – a world of all-night bars and street crime. Concerts weren't always easy. On some nights, John had to push people off the stage. To keep audiences happy, bands had to play well for six or seven hours every night. With all this practice, the band became better and better.

John Lennon:
'I grew up in Hamburg, not Liverpool.'

Another of the Liverpool bands in Hamburg was called Rory Storm and the Hurricanes. The band was famous in Liverpool. The band's drummer loved to come and watch the Beatles. Sometimes, when Pete Best was ill, he even played with the band. His name was Ringo Starr.

The first trip to Hamburg ended suddenly. George was sent home by the police because he was too young to play in the clubs – he was only seventeen. But the Beatles returned often to Hamburg. Each time they played to bigger crowds in better clubs.

In The Cavern

On their second trip to Hamburg, a record producer asked the Beatles to play on a record for the singer Tony Sheridan. The song was 'My Bonnie Lies Over the Ocean' and they played as the Beat Brothers. The boys were becoming successful. But one of the band decided that he didn't want to be a Beatle.

Stu met a young photographer, Astrid Kirchherr, in Hamburg. Her photos of the band later became famous. She also helped the band's look. One day, she cut Stu's hair. At first, the others in the band laughed – they all pushed their hair back off their faces like rock and roll singers. But later John, Paul and George all had the same haircut. After the band's second trip to Hamburg, Stu decided to stay there. He was in love with Astrid and he wanted to study art in Hamburg.

One of Astrid Kirchherr's famous photos with (from left to right) Pete, George, John, Paul and Stu

Paul never had a high opinion of Stu's playing, and he started to play the bass. Back in Liverpool, people were interested in the new band 'from Hamburg'. At first, someone told John, 'You speak good English.' But the band became more and more popular in their home city. They often played at a club called The Cavern. Hundreds of fans crowded into the small, dark club when the Beatles played there.

The band was famous now in Liverpool, but was that enough? Everything changed when they met Brian Epstein. He was the manager of a big music shop in the city. When he heard about the Beatles, he went to The Cavern. In his suit and tie, Epstein probably looked very different from The Cavern's young crowd. In his opinion, the band were a little rough. But, he has said, 'I immediately liked what I heard.' Epstein met the band and offered to become their manager. When he promised to make an agreement with a record company, the band said yes!

Brian Epstein immediately gave the band new rules. They couldn't eat, drink or smoke on stage. The four young men started wearing suits. Epstein worked hard for the band and on the last day of 1962, they drove down to London. They played for Decca, a big record company, but it didn't go well. Two months later, the company said no to Brian Epstein and the Beatles. In their opinion, guitar bands weren't popular now.

Worse news came from Germany. Stu was ill with terrible headaches. He died in April 1962, a day before the Beatles' third trip to Hamburg. He was only twenty-one.

During the band's third trip to Hamburg, they received a message from their manager. Another record company, Parlophone – part of the big company EMI – wanted to hear them in the studio.

On Their Way!

In June 1962, the Beatles were in London again – this time, at the Abbey Road studios. George Martin was one of the producers who was listening to them for the record company. Martin didn't like their songs much, but he liked the boys. After the Beatles finished playing, he showed them around the studio. The band were quiet.

'Is there anything you don't like?' asked Martin.

Finally, George spoke. 'Well, I don't like your tie.'

The fifth Beatle?

Before the Beatles, the producer George Martin mainly produced records of funny songs. But Martin knew a lot about music and about recording. Over the years, he helped the Beatles to grow as musicians. At first, he was really the boss. But after a time, the band told him what they wanted.

George Martin with Paul and John in the studio

A few weeks later, Martin called Brian Epstein. Yes, the band could make a record with him . . . but not with Pete Best on drums. In the producer's opinion, Pete wasn't good enough. It was a hard decision for the band, but Pete had to go. The drummer was angry when Brian Epstein told him the news.

The next decision was easier. In Paul's words, they wanted 'the greatest drummer in Liverpool' – their friend from Hamburg, Ringo Starr. Epstein called Ringo on a Wednesday and asked him to join the band. By Saturday, Ringo was the new drummer. Some fans weren't happy about the change. At The Cavern, a few people shouted angrily and held up signs: 'Pete is Best!'

The married Beatle

Before they went back to London John married his girlfriend, Cynthia. Marriage to a Beatle wasn't easy. John was often away from home. When their son Julian was born in 1963, fans even ran after John at the hospital. Later, the Beatles didn't want their young fans to know that one of the band was married. After their first tour of the US, a reporter asked John, 'Did your wife like the country?' John joked, 'Who? Who?'

The band recorded their first single, 'Love Me Do', at Abbey Road in September 1962. It was one of Paul's songs. Fans wrote to radio stations, asking them to play the record. By December 1962, the song was quite successful at number seventeen.* The Beatles were on their way!

· ·

*number seventeen: the seventeenth most popular single that week. (Every band wanted to reach number one.)

Beatlemania

It was time to choose a song for the important second record. George Martin didn't like any of John and Paul's songs at the time, so he chose a new song. The group said no. They wanted to do one of their songs. Today many bands write their own songs, but at the time this was a brave decision for a new band.

Finally, Martin agreed to record one of John's songs, 'Please Please Me'. At first it was a slow song, but the producer asked them to play it faster. After they recorded it, Martin told them, 'You have just recorded your first number one.'

The Beatles worked hard to make this true. They drove all over Britain to concerts. Sometimes they stopped the van to listen to their own song on the radio. Once the van was freezing after the front window broke. The Beatles lay together in the back to keep warm!

In March 1963, 'Please Please Me' reached number one. George Martin was right. After that, number one followed number one. Their singles in 1963 were 'From Me to You', 'She Loves You' and 'I Want to Hold Your Hand'.

Suddenly, everybody loved the Beatles. When the band played in concert, police had to hold back crowds of screaming fans – mainly girls. One newspaper thought of a new word to describe the country's love of the boys from Liverpool – 'Beatlemania'! Every Beatles single reached number one until 1967.

The band also recorded their first album early in 1963. George Martin asked them to come to the studio and play all the songs from their live show. They did this ... in one long day! The album *Please Please Me* was recorded in about twelve hours. It went to number one, too.

One of the Beatles' most famous songs from the first album wasn't written by Lennon and McCartney. They recorded the rock and roll song 'Twist and Shout' (by Phil Medley and Bert Russell) at the end of that long day. Everyone loved John's voice on the song. In fact, he was very tired at the time. 'I was just screaming,' he remembered later. ───────────────────

They recorded their second album later in the same year. *With the Beatles* still had rock and roll songs like Chuck Berry's 'Roll Over Beethoven', but Lennon and McCartney wrote more songs for the album. The cover's black-and-white photo became famous. They asked the photographer to copy Astrid's photos of the band in Hamburg.

Beatlemania

'America was ours!'

The Beatles were selling millions of records in Britain. *The Sunday Times* newspaper compared Lennon and McCartney with Beethoven. But many of the group's fans had other things on their minds. A lot of young fans dreamt about their favourite Beatle:

- **Paul** was the sweet, romantic one.
- **George** was the quiet one.
- **Ringo** was the happy, funny one.
- **John** was the intelligent one. He often made jokes, but they weren't always kind.

Follow the leader

In the very early days, John was the band's leader. When the band became successful, his position wasn't so clear. Both he and Paul wrote songs and sang for the band. In front of the cameras, Paul often spoke for the band, but John usually had the last word. To George, John was always the strongest person in the group. Years after John's death, he said, 'I think he is still the leader now, probably.'

At the beginning of 1964, the Beatles were the most popular band in Britain. They were famous in Europe, but they were still a little nervous about the United States. Many English stars looked for success across the Atlantic before the Beatles, but failed.

The Beatles' first singles in the US didn't do very well. But interest grew, and finally 'I Want to Hold Your Hand' reached number one. The band flew there in February 1964. They all knew how important this trip was. In Ringo's words, America was all that they dreamt about years earlier.

The trip was a big success. When the band played on TV's *The Ed Sullivan Show*, they were watched by an American TV audience of almost seventy-three million people. It was one of the most important shows in the history of popular music. The Beatles played in Washington and Miami, and went home happy. As Ringo said, 'America was ours now.' The band were world stars.

The Beatles returned to the United States later in 1964, as part of a big world tour. This trip was as successful as the last one. Ringo remembers that 'it was just so much fun.' As usual, nobody could hear the music at the concerts because of the screams of the fans. At this time it wasn't a big problem for the band, but it became more and more important later. George's memory of this tour was less happy than Ringo's. President Kennedy was killed only a year before, and George didn't want anyone to shoot one of the Beatles.

The Beatles on The Ed Sullivan Show

Up and Up

After the first American tour, the Beatles turned to another world – films. They made *A Hard Day's Night* in the spring of 1964. The title of the film and the song of the same name was something that Ringo said. The rest of the band often laughed at the drummer's unusual way of saying things.

The film's writer, Alan Owen, spent a few days with the band. The Beatles were funny, and the film showed this. Owen also understood the band's daily life. For much of the film, they were running away from screaming fans. The band liked making the film, but George probably enjoyed it most. He fell in love with one of the actresses, Patti Boyd. They were married in 1966.

John, Ringo, George and Paul in A Hard Day's Night

The black-and-white film was first shown in London and Liverpool. It was a big success. (The album was, too. This time, all the songs were by Lennon and McCartney.) Many people really liked Ringo's acting in the film. Some even called him 'the new Charlie Chaplin'. But Ringo remembers that he came straight from a club for one very funny part. He says that he wasn't acting much!

John and Paul's musical ideas were growing all the time. Each new song was different and exciting.

A different sound

John and Paul were both big fans of Bob Dylan's music. The subjects and language in the young American's songs were always unusual and interesting. The song 'I'm a Loser' on the album *Beatles for Sale*, at the end of 1964, sounded a little like a Dylan song. The same was true of the following year's 'You've Got to Hide Your Love Away'.

John even found time to write a book in 1964. *John Lennon In His Own Write* was full of funny short stories and pictures. It didn't have any serious meaning. In the introduction Paul wrote, 'If it seems funny, then that's enough.' John wrote another book the next year.

In early 1965, the Beatles made their second film. After the success of *A Hard Day's Night*, there was more money. But the band just wanted to travel and have a good time. 'We started saying, "We've never been to the Bahamas. Could you write that in?"' Paul remembers. As George said later, 'We had fun in those days.' But John remembered it differently. This wasn't a happy time for him. 'You can't see it but I'm singing "Help!"' he said.

'Here to stay'

Later in 1965, Paul wrote one of the most popular songs of all time. 'Yesterday' was a beautiful, sad song about lost love.

STORY BEHIND THE SONG ■ ■ ■ ■
The music for 'Yesterday' came to Paul in a dream. He 'just woke up one morning' with the song in his head. At first, he thought it was an old song. But none of his friends knew it. The first words to the song were about eggs!

George Martin loved the song immediately. But, in his opinion, it needed something different. Paul recorded it without the rest of the band. He played the guitar alone, while a small group of musicians played strings.

The song is one of the band's most famous – it has been recorded by many different singers and groups and in many different ways. Paul was sometimes angry when people called it their favourite Beatles song.

Paul sings 'Yesterday'

The King and the Queen

In August, the Beatles were back in the United States. Fifty-six thousand fans saw them at a concert in New York. At the time, it was the biggest concert crowd ever. The concert was exciting, but Ringo's memories of it weren't good. At times John was joking too much on stage, in Ringo's opinion.

Also, not many people at the concert really heard the band. Like most Beatles concerts, the sound of the crowd was louder than the music. The Beatles couldn't hear much of the music either. So, of course, it was difficult to play well.

'I always wanted to play with good players,' remembers Ringo. But now the band was playing badly on stage, and nobody was listening.

On the same tour, the Beatles met one of their favourite singers – Elvis Presley. 'It was one of the great meetings of my life,' Paul has said.

The boys and the 'King' had a good time. But years later the band discovered that Elvis was worried about the Beatles' success in his country. He asked the American government to send them home.

Back in Britain, the government gave all the Beatles the MBE. This award was often given to successful businesspeople or to people who fought bravely for their country. Many Britons were angry. How could the government give this award to a pop group? But the usual crowd of screaming fans were outside Buckingham Palace when the Queen gave them the award in October 1965. The Beatles were nervous – George later remembered that they rested and had a cigarette in the toilets in Buckingham Palace!

Rubber Soul

The next album, *Rubber Soul*, came out in December 1965. It was another big step for the band. They were exploring different kinds of music and different subjects. 'In My Life' was a beautiful song about places and people in the past. Even the album's love songs weren't the simple love songs of the band's early days.

One of the most interesting songs on the album was John's 'Norwegian Wood'. Many people wanted to know what the song meant. It was about a girl, but he didn't want his wife Cynthia to know this. George played the Indian musical instrument the *sitar* on 'Norwegian Wood'. He first noticed the instrument in an Indian restaurant in the film *Help!*. This was the start of George's long interest in Indian music and ideas.

STORY BEHIND THE SONG ■ ■ ■ ■

Around the time of *Rubber Soul*, the single 'Day Tripper' / 'We Can Work It Out' reached number one. Paul wrote most of 'We Can Work It Out' and John wrote the middle part. This song showed the differences between the two men clearly. The main part was more hopeful, as Paul sang, 'Try to see it my way . . .' John's part of the song was less hopeful: 'Life is very short and there's no time . . .'

The band's success continued with Paul's 'Paperback Writer' in 1966. It was their first single that wasn't about love. The music was becoming less and less simple, too. But now the Beatles faced a new problem – how could they play the songs in concert?

'Beatles go home!'

In June 1966, the Beatles were in Hamburg again to begin a new tour. Then they flew to Tokyo and the tour began to go wrong. There were many Beatles fans in Japan. But some people there thought the group was a bad example to young people. The band had to stay in their hotel. They only came out to play in concert.

Things became worse in the Philippines. In George's words, it was 'bad news' from the beginning. The real problem came after the concert in Manila. Imelda Marcos, the wife of the country's leader, invited the band to a party. The band's answer was a polite no. (Some of them can't even remember the invitation.)

The next day, something was clearly wrong. Nobody at the hotel brought breakfast for the band. Then they turned on the television and suddenly they understood: they saw Imelda Marcos in tears! The camera showed crying children and the empty dinner table. In George's words, 'We watched ourselves not arriving.'

The people of the Philippines were very angry. As the band drove to the airport, crowds shouted, 'Beatles go home!' The band was pushed around at the airport and their road manager was knocked over. Before they could leave, Brian Epstein was called off the aeroplane. He had to give back all the money from the band's concert there. Years later, Paul knew more about Marcos's government. Then he was happy about missing the garden party. Ringo has said about the country, 'I've never been back . . .'

The Sound of the Future

The 1966 tour wasn't a happy one, but in the studio that year the band were going into exciting new areas. George Martin had to find newer and newer sounds to record the band's ideas. The album *Revolver* was his favourite. The album was important for all the Beatles in different ways:

George was growing as a song writer. At first, it was difficult for the guitarist. His very early songs weren't strong, and he was in a band with two of the most famous songwriters in the world. In *Revolver*'s 'Love You To', he showed his continuing interest in Indian music. His best song on the album was probably 'Taxman'.

The band liked **Ringo** to sing a song on every album. Paul decided to give the drummer a song that wasn't very serious. He thought of 'Yellow Submarine' one night in bed.

Paul continued to write about new subjects and to explore new kinds of music. 'Eleanor Rigby' was a sad song about the lives of lonely people in a big city. Again, strings were used, and McCartney recorded the song without the other Beatles. 'We were just drinking tea,' said George.

John was exploring, too. With the songs 'She Said She Said' and 'Tomorrow Never Knows', he went into strange new musical areas. 'Tomorrow Never Knows' was like a promise of the wild music at the end of the 1960s. Listen to this song and compare it to any song from the Beatles' first two or three albums. A lot changed in those few years!

Burning Records

In 1966, John spoke to a reporter in London. They were talking about the modern church, and he said, 'We're more popular than Jesus now.' When John's words were reported in the US a few months later, many people were angry. There were newspaper stories like 'Lennon Says that the Beatles are Bigger than Jesus'. This wasn't what John meant. But some shops refused to sell their records. Some radio stations refused to play them. A few radio stations asked listeners to burn their Beatles records. Years later, Ringo joked, 'It was OK for us, because then they bought them again!' But at the time, the band and their manager were worried.

John and Paul talk to reporters

So what did John mean? He tried to explain his words to the American people before the band toured the country again. 'I was just saying it as a fact,' he explained. 'It is true – more for England than here. I'm not saying that we're better or greater ... I'm sorry that I opened my mouth.'

It was a bad start to the Beatles' last tour.

The End of Touring

The tour continued, but it wasn't a happy time. Some newspapers in the United States were against the band now. For the first time, there were a few empty seats at some concerts. But it was still impossible to hear the music because of the screams. As George said, touring wasn't 'fun' now. Also, their lives were different. Only one Beatle – Paul – wasn't married. It was time to stop travelling.

At first, Paul wanted to tour more, but finally he agreed with the others. On 29 August 1966, they played at Candlestick Park in San Francisco. They played eleven songs, finishing with 'I'm Down'. It was the Beatles' last concert.

The band faced a new question: what now? In his heart, John thought, 'This is the end, really.'

For some time the Beatles all did different things:

■ **George** spent a few weeks in India.

■ **Paul** worked with George Martin on the music for a film, *The Family Way*. The music won an award.

■ **John** went to Spain to act in a film, *How I Won the War*. It wasn't a good film, and John wasn't a good actor. But he did come back wearing the famous small, round 'John Lennon glasses'!

■ **Ringo** spent a few weeks in Spain with John, and he enjoyed time at home with his wife and child.

Back in the studio, the band felt more free. Now they didn't have to play any new songs on stage. They could do anything, and they did – with George Martin's help. The next songs were another big step into new musical areas. But they also looked back, as both John and Paul turned to their Liverpool past for 'Strawberry Fields Forever' and 'Penny Lane'.

STORY BEHIND THE SONGS ■ ■ ■ ■

• When he was a child, John lived near a children's home. The home was called Strawberry Field. John's song 'Strawberry Fields Forever' wasn't really about that place; it just took the home's name. The line 'Nothing is real' perfectly described this strange, beautiful song.

• Paul then wrote a song about Liverpool, too. 'Penny Lane' was a much happier song, describing people and places from the old days in Liverpool. The band was still using instruments that were unusual in pop records. A trumpet played on the song. _____

There were many differences between Paul and John. Paul was very interested in studio recording. He worked carefully with George Martin. John had little time for this. He just told the producer what he wanted. In fact, the band played 'Strawberry Fields Forever' in two very different ways. John couldn't choose his favourite. Finally, the producer joined the two. (Years later, John wasn't happy about this recording of his song.)

Together, 'Strawberry Fields Forever' and 'Penny Lane' became the Beatles' next single. It was a great record, but for the first time in years the band didn't reach number one.

The Most Famous Album in the World

In the opinion of some newspapers in early 1967, the Beatles didn't have any more ideas. And then came *Sergeant Pepper's Lonely Hearts Club Band*.

The title song was Paul's. He had the idea after a trip to the United States. Bands with very long names were becoming popular there. Paul wanted the Beatles to be a different band for the album. In his mind, the album was a concert by this other band.

John and George didn't see the album in this way. 'It doesn't go anywhere,' John once said about the *Sergeant Pepper* idea. But there were great songs on the album.

* Songs like 'When I'm Sixty-Four' and 'With a Little Help From My Friends' were happy and light.

* John took almost all the words for 'Being for the Benefit of Mr Kite' from an old sign that he found in a shop.

* The words and the music of 'Lucy in the Sky With Diamonds' were like a dream. The title came from a picture by John's young son, Julian.

* 'A Day in the Life' was one of the best examples of Paul and John's strong points. John wrote the main part of the song, beginning 'I read the news today, oh boy.' The idea came from two newspaper stories. Paul added the middle part. It worked perfectly in John's song.

The album was a big step in the band's music. They used the studio wonderfully, but this took a long time. The Beatles' first album was made in around twelve hours, but *Sergeant Pepper* took over 700 hours! Both Ringo and George said later that it was sometimes boring. 'My heart was still in India,' George said.

24

Famous faces

Everything about the album was special – even the cover. It showed the band with a crowd of famous people – writers, singers, actors, thinkers. At first there was a photo of Mahatma Gandhi, but the record company asked the band to take it off. They didn't want to make people in India angry.

Today, fans disagree about which is the best Beatles album. But most of them believe that *Sergeant Pepper* was the most important. The world was changing fast in 1967. While the American war in Vietnam continued, young people around the world were exploring new ideas, new sounds. The summer of 1967 became known as 'the summer of love'. *Sergeant Pepper* helped to make that summer.

Life and Death

Not long after *Sergeant Pepper*, the Beatles were invited to play in a live television programme called *Our World*. Different countries had to make different parts of the show, and the makers of the programme wanted the Beatles to play for Britain's part. John wrote the song and on 25 June 1967, about 350 million people all around the world watched the programme.

The Beatles weren't alone in the television studio. A lot of other musicians played and it was like a big party. Eric Clapton and Mick Jagger were both there. John's song was perfect for the programme: 'All You Need Is Love' was a mirror for the dreams and hopes of young people around the world in 1967.

The Beatles play on Our World

At the end of 'All You Need Is Love', the Beatles joked about two of their old songs. John sang 'Yesterday' and Paul sang a line from 'She Loves You'. _____

Around this time, George was continuing to learn more about Eastern ideas. He asked John and Paul to listen to a talk by the Maharishi Mahesh Yogi in London. The Maharishi was an Indian who taught Eastern ways of thinking.

The Beatles wanted to know more. In August, all four of them took a train to Bangor in North Wales. They wanted to spend a few days studying with the Maharishi.

A sad sign

Cynthia Lennon wanted to go too, but the usual Beatles crowds were at the train station and Cynthia missed the train. She watched as her husband left without her. For her, this was a sign of the end of their marriage.

While the Beatles were searching for the meaning of life, sad news reached them from London. Brian Epstein was dead. 'He was one of us,' John told a reporter.

Brian Epstein

On the Bus

Epstein's death brought another problem. The Beatles knew nothing about business. 'We were in trouble then,' said John. Ringo has described the band as 'chickens without heads' at that time. In the middle of this difficult time, Paul had an idea. He wanted to make a television film. He was trying to help the band, but in John and George's opinion, Paul was trying to lead them.

The idea for the film was simple. Forty-three people – with the Beatles – drove around the country in a bus. This time, they didn't have a story to act. They just filmed what happened. There was one problem – nothing really did happen.

Magical Mystery Tour was shown on television in Britain just after Christmas, 1967. Almost fifteen million people watched. They loved the songs, like Paul's 'The Fool on the Hill' and John's 'I Am the Walrus'. But not many people liked the film. The colour film was shown in black and white on television. But this wasn't the reason why it wasn't popular. For some people it was boring, for others it was too strange. For the first time, the Beatles really failed.

STORY BEHIND THE SONG ■ ■ ■ ■
The idea for 'I Am The Walrus' came from Lewis Carroll's book *Alice in Wonderland*. John said, 'The words don't say a lot ...'

In February 1968, the Beatles travelled to India to study again with the Maharishi. The trip had a different meaning for each of them. Ringo went with two suitcases – one of clothes and one of English food in tins! He didn't stay long. Paul says that he enjoyed this time in India. But John and George stayed longer. George continued to defend the Maharishi, but John soon became angry at their old teacher. A song on the band's next album was an angry attack on him.

Back in Britain, there were no simple answers in business for the Beatles. They opened the Apple shop in London. Paul called it 'a beautiful place where you can buy beautiful things'. The shop lost money almost immediately. But Apple was more than a shop. It was a big company that produced music and films. The Beatles began to produce other musicians. Paul was most interested in Apple's business. He was there more because he lived in London. But the others felt that Paul was trying to lead the band again.

Yellow Submarine

In July 1968, there was another Beatles film in cinemas. The band recorded a few new songs for *Yellow Submarine*, but they didn't even do the voices in the film. In the story, the band saved a strange place called Pepperland with their music.

A New Album and a New Love

In 1968, Cynthia and John Lennon's marriage ended. John was with Yoko Ono now. He first met the Japanese–American artist at an art show in 1966 and they slowly fell in love.

STORY BEHIND THE SONG ■ ■ ■ ■ ■
Paul felt sorry for Cynthia and Julian Lennon. The boy was only five. Paul wrote a song for him. He later changed the words from 'Hey Jules' to 'Hey Jude'.

Everything changed for John with Yoko. He often spoke of her as his teacher. Together they explored new ideas. These were called crazy by many people, but John and Yoko weren't worried. They made their first record together in one night. It was an exploration of sounds. But the biggest news was the cover. It showed John and Yoko without any clothes. 'We just wanted to be together all the time,' remembered John.

John and Yoko were together in the studio, too, as the Beatles started their next album. This soon became a problem for the

other Beatles. Ringo asked him, 'What's this all about?' The other two and George Martin were angrier. When Yoko was ill, John even brought a bed into the studio for her!

In 1968 the Beatles' *White Album* had other problems. Ringo left the band for a time. (The band recorded a few songs without him.) In his opinion, the other Beatles didn't need him. When they all asked him back, the drummer returned happily. 'I loved the *White Album*,' he remembers now.

But not everyone had this opinion. John spoke about the start of the band's 'slow death' at this time. The musical interests in the band were more and more different. The Beatles were less and less a real group. Sometimes the album was recorded in three different studios at the same time, as John, Paul and George worked on their own songs.

The double album mixed many different kinds of music. 'Ob-La-Di, Ob-La-Da' was a happy pop song, while 'Revolution 9' was a strange piece of 'sound art'. In 'Back in the USSR' the band cleverly sounded like the Beach Boys. George's best song on the album was probably 'While My Guitar Gently Weeps'. His friend Eric Clapton joined the band to play on this song.

Secret messages • • • • • • • • • • • • • • • •
Two songs from the album later became famous for the wrong reasons. In the mind of Californian Charles Manson, the songs 'Piggies' and 'Helter Skelter' were secret messages telling him to kill.

George Martin thought that there were too many different songs on the double album. He wanted it to be an excellent single album. But Paul has said, 'It's a fine little album.' John also liked the simpler way of recording.

An Unhappy Film and Two Weddings

At the start of 1969, the band needed new plans. Paul was full of ideas for the band's future. They decided to write an album and then play it on stage – all in front of cameras. This was the start of *Let It Be*.

It was a bad time. The band weren't happy together, and all the cameras made everything worse. George even left the band for a short time after angry words with Paul. Things only got better when a guest musician, American Billy Preston, joined them.

The cameras filmed everything. The cameramen didn't know it at the time, but in fact they were recording the end of the group. The film *Let It Be* is difficult to watch at times.

The idea of a big concert soon died. Looking for a way to end the film, the band decided to play a few songs on the Apple building's roof. People in London looked up in surprise as the Beatles played 'Get Back' above them. For a short time, the old days were back! In Ringo's words, when the music was good, they forgot all the problems. Finally, the police asked the band to stop. They never played live together again.

Producer George Martin didn't want to touch the long *Let It Be* recordings. So American Phil Spector took the job. Finally, the *Let It Be* album came out after the end of the Beatles. Paul didn't like Spector's work on it. Both he and George Martin hated the strings on 'The Long and Winding Road'.

In 1969, Paul married for the first time and John married for the second time. Even the two marriages showed the differences between the two men.

Paul married American photographer Linda Eastman on 12 March. They wanted a quiet wedding, but nothing could be

Paul and Linda talk and laugh with Linda's daughter,
Heather, on their wedding day.

quiet for a Beatle. Hundreds of fans cried as Paul and his new
wife drove away.

Weeks later, John and Yoko were married in Gibraltar. The
story is told in the song 'The Ballad of John and Yoko'. Later,
they invited reporters to a 'bed-in' at their hotel. They stayed in
bed for seven days. They wanted people to think about the
meaning of love. (At a later 'bed-in', they recorded the song
'Give Peace a Chance'.)

John and Yoko gave their opinions on a lot of subjects, like
the Vietnam War. John sent his MBE back to the British
government. He had more and more interests in his life, and
the band wasn't one of them. But the Beatles stayed together
for one more record.

The Last Album

After the troubles on *Let It Be*, George Martin was surprised to receive a telephone call from Paul. The band wanted to make another album. Paul and Martin agreed to do one the 'old' way – in the studio. The album was named after the Abbey Road studio in London, and the Beatles worked on it there during July and August 1969.

John and Paul disagreed about some of their ideas for the album. Paul wanted to join all the songs together. John just liked to do different 'three-minute records'. To keep both men happy, only the songs on the second half of the record are joined together.

Abbey Road was a happy record to work on for most of the time. But not always. When Paul took three days to record 'Maxwell's Silver Hammer', George told him, 'It's only a song.'

STORY BEHIND THE SONG ■ ■ ■ ■

Abbey Road's 'Something' was the band's first single written by George Harrison. Many people think that it is his best song. Later, Frank Sinatra often sang it on stage. He described it as his favourite Lennon and McCartney song. Telling this story, Paul once joked, 'Thanks, Frank.'

Nobody knew it at the time, but *Abbey Road* was the last album. But the band ended it well. The last song was called 'The End'. John, Paul and George all played guitar on it. All four Beatles were playing together as a real band again. You can hear the fun in the music. Paul sang the last lines of the last album. They were about love.

Paul is dead!

After *Abbey Road* arrived in the shops in October 1969, a radio station in the US started a strange story about Paul. He was dead! The 'signs' were on the album's cover. Paul wasn't wearing shoes. In some countries, dead people are dressed in clothes but not shoes.

The story grew. The hand over Paul's head on the cover of *Sergeant Pepper* was, fans decided, a sign of death. A line in 'A Day in the Life' was also about Paul's death. More and more signs were found.

But if Paul was dead, who was the new person on the front of *Abbey Road*? The story became sillier. It was a man called William Campbell. Or it was Billy Shears (a singer's name from the title song on *Sergeant Pepper*). This new person looked exactly like Paul, of course.

Finally, *Life* magazine found Paul on his farm in Scotland. The magazine proved it. Paul wasn't dead. Paul described himself as 'the last to know' about his death.

Differences of Opinion

Even before *Abbey Road*, the Beatles' company Apple was losing a lot of money. Something had to change. They needed someone to manage the business.

John wanted Allan Klein, the manager of the Rolling Stones, to be the group's manager. George and Ringo agreed, but Paul didn't. He wanted Lee Eastman – his wife's father – to manage Apple's business.

Paul was still full of ideas for the band and the company, but it was too late. In one meeting, John spoke about the end of the Beatles: 'It feels good.'

In fact, Paul ended the band in 1970. A few weeks after his first album *McCartney* was in the shops, he told the world. He was leaving the Beatles 'because of personal, business and musical differences'.

The band was finished, but the fights about business and money continued in court for years. It was a sad end for the greatest band in the world.

The Beatles – the greatest band in the world

Life After the Beatles

All four of the Beatles found success alone.

■ **Ringo** acted in a few films and he continued to make records. His 1973 album *Ringo* was a big success. All the other Beatles played on this album ... but not at the same time. Ringo is still playing and touring with his All Starr Band. Many of Ringo's famous friends from the world of music – and his son, Zak – have played in this band.

Many British children know and love Ringo for another reason. He was the voice of a train in a famous children's television programme!

■ **George** seemed happy to be away from the shadows of Lennon and McCartney. His 1970 album *All Things Must Pass* reached number one around the world. George's most famous song in the 1970s was 'My Sweet Lord', but he was taken to court because of it. In the court's opinion, part of it was copied from an old song. In the early 1980s, George also played in the Travelling Wilburys with Bob Dylan and Roy Orbison.

George became interested in films, but not as an actor. He produced films like Monty Python's *Life of Brian* and *Time Bandits*.

In 1999, someone failed to kill George in his home. But sadly, two years later, he died after a long illness.

■ **Paul** has had the most success after the Beatles. After the albums *McCartney* and *Ram*, he wanted to be in a real band again. In 1971 he started a new band, Wings, with his wife Linda and guitarist Denny Laine. At first, Wings drove all over Britain playing small concerts. It was like the old days of the Beatles again.

Wings

Wings soon became big. 1973's *Band on the Run* was Paul's most successful album. In 1977, the band recorded 'Mull of Kintyre'. This song sold more than any other single in Britain before that time. Wings ended in 1981, but Paul continued making records. In 1997, he was back at Buckingham Palace. He became Sir Paul McCartney.

Paul has sold millions of records since 1970, but one of his biggest successes was his happy family life with Linda and their children. Sadly, in 1998, Linda McCartney died. Paul now has another woman, Heather Mills, in his life.

■ **John** and Yoko moved to New York. They still spoke openly on many subjects, and at one time the American government wanted to throw him out of the country. Some of John's most interesting work was on his first two albums, *John Lennon / Plastic Ono Band* and *Imagine*. On the first album, John sang painfully honest songs about his mother's death. In another song, he sang the words, 'I don't believe in Beatles / I just believe in me.' The title song of *Imagine* is probably his most famous song.

Most people think that John's later work in the 1970s wasn't as good. For some time, John and Yoko weren't together. John called this his 'lost weekend', but it lasted eighteen months.

Back with Yoko, John didn't make music for a few years. He looked after their son, Sean. He returned to the recording studio in the summer of 1980 to make *Double Fantasy* with Yoko. Much of the album was about family life. One of the songs from the album, '(Just Like) Starting Over' was doing well when John was killed.

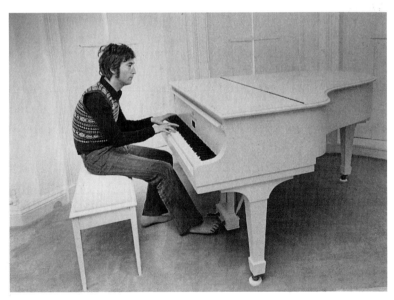

John sings 'Imagine'

Friends again

The Beatles ended badly, and some of the band were angry for a long time. On 1971's *Imagine*, John's song 'How Do You Sleep?' was an attack on Paul. (George Harrison was angry too – he played guitar on the song.)

But finally, Paul and John became friendlier again. Paul visited John a few times in New York after Sean Lennon's birth. In 1994, years after John's death, both men were given an important music award. On stage, Paul read out a letter to John. In it, he remembered their past together. He ended, 'This letter comes, with love, from your friend Paul.'

John and Paul in happy times

At the Top Again

The Beatles ruled the music world in the 1960s. They had twenty-two singles in Britain, and eighteen reached number one. Every album of new songs got to number one. In the United States, there were nineteen number one singles. Many people still think that they were the world's greatest band of all time. In one list of best albums, the top five were all by the Beatles!

But the band's success wasn't just for their musical past. In 1995, the three living Beatles came together to record two 'new' Beatles songs – 'Free as a Bird' and 'Real Love'. Both songs were by John. The singer recorded them, but they weren't finished. Paul, George and Ringo worked with these recordings, adding to them. In their minds, they were finishing the music for John while he worked on something else.

Fans could buy new Beatles records again! They also loved the video for 'Free as a Bird'. It showed people and places from the band's past – Stu Sutcliffe, Brian Epstein, The Cavern, the street outside the Abbey Road studios. There were hundreds of memories of Beatles songs. A few are:

- a cake with the number sixty-four ('When I'm Sixty-Four')
- a man writing a book ('Paperback Writer')
- a photo of Mao Tse Tung (a line from 'Revolution')
- a stone with the name Eleanor Rigby ('Eleanor Rigby')

At the same time, the living Beatles told their story in the television programme *The Beatles Anthology*. More than twenty million copies of the *Anthology* albums were sold. In 2000, there was a very successful album of the Beatles' number one songs. They made more money from the album than any other British artist that year. The Beatles were back in the right place – at the top!

ACTIVITIES

Pages 1–11

Before you read

1 What do you know about the Beatles? Do you have a favourite Beatles song?

2 Find these words in your dictionary. They are all used in this book.

   album   audience   band   concert   fan   rock and roll   single (n)   *studio   van*

   Which are words for:

   a   a type of music?

   b   recordings of music?

   c   a place where you record music?

   d   a group of musicians?

   e   hours of live music that you can buy tickets for?

   f   the people who watch and listen to musicians on stage?

   g   a person who loves a group and buys all its recordings?

   h   the vehicle that carries a group's musical equipment?

3 Work with another student. Find the words in *italics* in your dictionary.

   a   How do you play these? Show the movements.

      guitar/bass guitar   drum   trumpet

   b   Discuss the job of the person who *manages* a band. What does the manager do? Is it a good job, do you think?

   c   If you have a *mania* for something, do you like it or dislike it?

4 Discuss why the band's time in Hamburg was so important to them.

5 Work with another student. Have this conversation.

Student A: Imagine that you are with Pete Best. Ask him questions about his time with the band, and his feelings now about the Beatles.

Student B: You are Pete Best. Answer the questions.

Pages 12–25

Before you read

6 You are going to read about the Beatles' last tour. Why do you think that they stopped touring?

7 Find the words in *italics* in your dictionary. Then answer the questions.

a How many musical *instruments* can you name?

b How many of those instruments have *strings*?

8 Find the words below in your dictionary. Finish each sentence with one of the words.

award   explore   lead

a The band loved to ..... new sounds and new ideas.

b Most bands and singers are happy when they win an ..... .

c A band's songs are often written by the person who ..... the band.

After you read

9 What was so special about *Sergeant Pepper's Lonely Hearts Club Band*? Make a list of reasons.

10 Discuss the main differences between John Lennon and Paul McCartney.

Before you read

11 What do you know about the present lives and work of the Beatles who are still alive?

After you read

12 In Paul's opinion, he was trying to find new things for the band to do. To others, Paul was trying to be the leader of the band. Which do you think is true? Give reasons for your answer.

13 What was special about John and Yoko's marriage? Why do some people think that they were very unusual?

14 Discuss which Beatles album's story you find most interesting. Explain why.

Writing

15 Listen to a Beatles album. Choose two songs and write your opinion of them.

16 You are someone from the Beatles story (but not a Beatle). Write the introduction to *your* book about the band.

17 A friend doesn't know any Beatles songs. Write to them. Tell them what they should listen to.

18 Write a letter to one of the living Beatles or to Yoko Ono. Explain your feelings about the band.

Answers for the Activities in this book are available from your local Pearson Education office. Alternatively, write to: Marketing Department, Penguin Longman Publishing, 80 Strand, London WC2R 0RL.
Also visit www.penguinreaders.com for your free Factsheet for this book.